"Be unceasing in prayer [praying perseveringly]"
– *1 Thessalonians 5:17 (AMPC)*

For those seeking a deeper connection with God through prayer, devotion, and spiritual growth. May this prayer book guide you in aligning your heart with His will and inspire you to walk boldly in faith.

This book is designed to enrich your spiritual journey and deepen your relationship with God. Use it as a companion for your daily devotions, during moments of quiet meditation, or as a guide to strengthen your faith.

- Read the Prayers, Declarations, and Reflections: Allow the words to uplift, encourage, and align your heart with God's will.

- Meditate on the Scriptures: Take time to focus on the Word of God referenced throughout the book.

- Be Inspired by the Quotes: Let the carefully chosen quotes bring fresh insights and encouragement for your journey.

This book invites you to engage with its pages in faith and expectation, as you draw closer to God and embrace His purpose for your life.

A Prayerful Heart
PRAYERS | DECLARATIONS | REFLECTIONS

A Prayerful Heart: Prayers, Declarations & Reflections
Copyright © 2024 by Milagros Hayes, Diaraha R. McDaniels, and Jerrold Snipes. All rights reserved.

Prayers and declarations authored by Milagros Hayes (Ap. Milagros Hayes), Diaraha R. McDaniels (Prophetess Dee McDaniels), and Jerrold Snipes (Pastor Jerrold Snipes) are Copyright © 2024 by their respective authors and are used with permission.

Contributing Authors
- **Milagros Hayes**, Miracles Ministries (https://MiraclesMinistriesMovement.org)
- **Jerrold Snipes**, Legacy Fellowship (https://LF-SA.org)
- **Diaraha R. McDaniels**, D. R. McDaniels Ministries (https://DRMcDEnterprise.com)

No part of this publication may be reproduced, stored, or transmitted in any form or by any means—electronic, mechanical, photocopying, recording, or otherwise—without prior written permission from the publisher, except for brief quotations in reviews, scholarly analysis, or personal devotional use.

Scripture References
- Scripture quotations marked AMPC are taken from the Amplified® Bible, Classic Edition, Copyright © 1954, 1958, 1962, 1964, 1965, 1987 by The Lockman Foundation. Used by permission. www.lockman.org
- Scripture quotations marked NIV are taken from the Holy Bible, New International Version®, NIV®. Copyright © 1973, 1978, 1984, 2011 by Biblica, Inc.® Used by permission. All rights reserved worldwide. Learn more at www.Biblica.com.
- Scripture quotations marked KJV are taken from the King James Version of the Bible, which is in the public domain.

ISBN
979-8-9877971-3-6 (Prayer Book)
979-8-9877971-1-2 (Spiral Bound Journal)
979-8-9877971-2-9 (Perfect Bound Journal)

Publisher
DRM Publishing, LLC
4580 Klahanie Dr. SE, PMB 153
Issaquah, WA 98029
drmpublishingllc@gmail.com | (726) 243-9996

Cover Design, Book Design, and Composition
D'Opus Creative Design Solutions
A division of D'Opus Agency, LLC
https://www.dopusagency.com

Edited By
Dylann S. Smith and Diaraha R. McDaniels (Overall Editors)
Contributions were reviewed for accuracy and alignment by Milagros Hayes and Jerrold Snipes.

Edition
First Edition, 2024

Printed in the United States of America

DRM Publishing, LLC

"To be a Christian without prayer is no more possible than to be alive without breathing."

– *Martin Luther*

The Journey...

Prayers & Declarations

Prayers & Intercessions

Reflections: Peace, Praise & Worship

Reflections: Whispers of the Soul©

Declarations
Prayers & Declarations

Philippians 4:6

"You can do more than pray after you have prayed, but you cannot do more than pray until you have prayed."
– *John Bunyan*

Prayer & Declaration: Good Morning Prayer

Father, in the name of Jesus, I thank You for Your divine protection, provision, favor, goodness, and mercy upon my life and the life of every family member and friend. Holy Spirit, I yield to Your divine guidance, wisdom, knowledge, counsel, understanding, might, and fear of the Lord this day. Father, thank You for Your ministering angels assigned to my life; thank You that they are active and on assignment to guard, protect, and minister to me and my family in the name of Jesus.

I declare the peace of God upon my day. I declare favor upon my life. I declare grace upon grace. In the name of Jesus, I thank You for the manifestation of the Spirit's power wherever I go. What I put my hands to do is blessed, and wherever my feet touch is blessed. I live in Christ's abundant joy, which is my strength.

Father, thank You for going before me and Your glory being my rear guard.

Thank You, Lord, for hiding me in the secret place of the Most High, where I abide under the shadow of the Almighty!

In Jesus' name, Amen

Ap. Milagros Hayes
Miracles Ministries

Prayer & Declaration: Daily Prayer

Lord, I commit my day to Your plans. I yield my spirit, soul, and body to Your perfect will and purpose in my life, marriage, family, business, and ministry.

I surrender to serve You with clean hands and a pure heart.

I surrender my will to live a life of unconditional love and to be intentional today in sharing your love with family, friends, and all I encounter.

Thank You for leading me by Your Spirit and anointing me to fulfill this day's assignments.

I declare this day will manifest on Earth as it is in Heaven. In Jesus' name, Amen

Ap. Milagros Hayes
Miracles Ministries

Prayer & Declaration

May the Lord bless you and keep you! May He shine His face upon you! May you experience the favor of the Lord today! May He lead and guide you as He deposits strategies within you. May His grace be present in your life. May His angels protect you and your family. May your prayers, offered in faith, be answered. May you come to know Him even more deeply. May your words and thoughts align with His will and manifest in your life. May the blessing of Abraham be upon you. May His love overwhelm you. Be blessed!

Numbers 6:24-26 (AMPC)
The Lord bless you and watch, guard, and keep you; The Lord make His face to shine upon and enlighten you and be gracious (kind, merciful, and giving favor) to you; The Lord lift up His [approving] countenance upon you and give you peace (tranquility of heart and life continually).

Prophetess Dee McDaniels
D. R. McDaniels Ministries

Prayer & Declaration

May the God of Peace manifest in your life, home, and family. May His grace sustain you always. I pray that you and your family experience His favor and love in ways that leave you astonished.

May His love overwhelm your heart, providing security and peace beyond understanding. May He guide your decisions with wisdom from His Word and supply all you need to fulfill His purpose for your life.

I pray that you see answers to your prayers and witness His hand in the matters that concern you most. May His favor draw others to you, and may your soul find rest and unspeakable joy in Him.

May the blessing of Abraham rest upon your family, bringing deliverance and salvation to all who need Him. May your loved ones, near and far, come to a saving knowledge of Jesus Christ.

May you be strengthened in your inner being and refreshed by His Spirit. Walk in His love and grace all the days of your life. Amen.

Prophetess Dee McDaniels
D. R. McDaniels Ministries

Prayer & Declaration

May the Lord of the Breakthrough go before you, shattering every obstacle and stronghold (2 Samuel 5:20). May His peace, which surpasses all understanding, guard your heart and mind in Christ Jesus (Philippians 4:7). May His manifested presence and power rest upon you, bringing transformation to your life and those around you (Romans 12:2).

May the sound of His presence through you shift every atmosphere, silencing confusion and bringing His order and glory (Psalm 29:3-4). May you dwell in the secret place of the Most High and find refuge under His wings all the days of your life (Psalm 91:1). May your children and their children be rooted and established in His love and know His mighty power at work within them (Ephesians 3:17-18).

May His angels encamp around you, protecting and delivering you from harm (Psalm 34:7). May His grace and anointing flow through your life, drawing others to His salvation and revealing His glory on earth (Matthew 5:16).

May His love, overflowing in your heart, pour out as a testimony, leading many to the saving knowledge of Jesus Christ (John 13:35). May you witness the fulfillment of every prayer and promise according to His Word, for His glory and your good (2 Corinthians 1:20).

Be blessed and strengthened as you walk in the power of His breakthrough!

Prophetess Dee McDaniels
D. R. McDaniels Ministries

Prayer & Declaration

Father, Thank You for the new beginning. I receive Your abundant life, the cleansing and the washing by the word of God. I receive the riches of Your glory in Christ Jesus. I declare that the Spirit of God empowers us to speak the word of God boldly. Thank You, Father, for Your grace upon us and the fullness of Your life that dwells within us. Hallelujah in the name of Jesus, Amen.

Ap. Milagros Hayes
Miracles Ministries

Prayer & Declaration: Paradigm Shift

I pray for inner strength by the power of the Holy Spirit to break through the consciousness of this world's limits that hinder my spiritual progress. I declare Your power is shifting my mind into divine alignment with the Kingdom of God. In the name of Yeshua, Amen.

Ap. Milagros Hayes
Miracles Ministries

Prayer & Prophetic Declaration:
Kingdom Marketplace

Father, Thank You for blessing me and anointing me to excel in the Marketplace. Thank You for the intelligence that navigates and operates in me to manifest the excellency of Your Kingdom on earth as in Heaven. I declare I am empowered in both the spiritual and natural realms as an Ambassador of Christ. Thank You for divine protection in hostile work environments. You have graced me with a Kingly Anointing to reign, succeed, and advance Your Kingdom. I am anointed to set at liberty those enslaved in the world system!!! Wherever my feet step, it is blessed, what I put my hands to do is blessed. You have empowered my spirit to command forth Atmospheric Shifts from bondage to Kingdom Dominion.

Prophetic Declaration
You are about to press beyond the gates of this realm and into the Kingly dimensions in Heavenly Places. That is where access to the keys you need are located for earthly breakthroughs.

continues on next page...

Father, by Your anointing, yokes are destroyed, burdens are removed, and curses are reversed. we bind the slave task masters' captivity off of our families, friends, co-workers, ministries, and businesses. We pull down demonic structures and strongholds of enslavement, we sever every tie to Babylonian beliefs and power, and we release the wisdom, creativity, knowledge, and intelligence of the Spirit in our lives and every area of our destiny, our sons and daughters, we embrace the blessings of the new covenant and receive our inheritance. We call forth the transfer of wealth from Egypt to come into our possession. In Jesus' name, Amen.

Exodus 6:6-8 (NIV)
Therefore, say to the Israelites: 'I am the Lord, and I will bring you out from under the yoke of the Egyptians. I will free you from being slaves to them, and I will redeem you with an outstretched arm and with mighty acts of judgment. I will take you as my own people, and I will be your God. Then you will know that I am the Lord your God, who brought you out from under the yoke of the Egyptians. And I will bring you to the land I swore with uplifted hand to give to Abraham, to Isaac and to Jacob. I will give it to you as a possession. I am the Lord.'

Ap. Milagros Hayes
Miracles Ministries

Prayer & Declaration:
Leaders & Their Families

Holy and Righteous Father, I come before Your Throne of Grace as I lift up your leaders and their families, ministries, and businesses. I declare Your promises upon them and all You have given them to govern on the earth and in the heavens. I declare that the Power of the Spirit is demonstrated in everything they put their hands to do. Thank You for the increase, expansion, grace, ability, knowledge, and understanding to administrate effectively in those areas. I break cycles and thought patterns that challenge our Kingdom movements and declare divine shifting by the Holy Spirit and Your Word. Release Christ's mind and the revelation of the Spirit into each life so that greater light will emanate from their being as Jesus on the Mount of Transfiguration. Today is a Great Day! Today is a Glorious Day! Today is a Prosperous and Successful Day! Today Is a Spirit-led day in the name of Yeshua!! Amen.

Ap. Milagros Hayes
Miracles Ministries

Intercession

Prayer & Intercession

Ephesians 6:18

"The intercessor must become responsible for the prayer that the Holy Spirit gives them. They must 'pray through' until the prayer is answered."

– *Reese Howells*

Prayer & Intercession
Hebrews 7:25

Father, the cries of Your heart have become the cries of our hearts. Father, Your eyes behold everything upon the earth, and You feel the pain of the oppressed, sick, downtrodden, the lonely, and those in despair. The weight and burden of Your heart no human can bear. We ask You for Your grace and ability to intercede on behalf of the many requests that come before Your Throne. Holy Spirit, refresh every intercessor in this season who has labored between the porch and the altar. We need a refreshing and renewed strength to continue in this labor of love to which we so willingly give our lives. Thank You, Father, for the honor of allowing us to co-labor with our King and Priest, whoever lives to make intercession for us. Messiah, we Love You!

Ap. Milagros Hayes
Miracles Ministries

Prayer

Holy Spirit, remove the veils within my soul, all that hinders You having Your way in my life. Lord, I desire to live upright that my life will bring You glory. I embrace and receive the purification that brings forth light in my being. I submit fully to the immersing of my entire spirit, soul, and body in your transformation. His light shines bright from within me in Jesus' name!

Ap. Milagros Hayes
Miracles Ministries

Prayer & Exhortation

I pray the eyes of your heart be enlightened to the truth of God's word, may Christ's love flourish in your lives, and may His light and glory shine brightly in you. I pray you bear fruit in every area of your life, family, business, community, ministries, and more.

Arise and shine, for the glory of the Lord has risen upon you. Love extravagantly, rejoice abundantly, and soak in His presence until His aroma fills the atmosphere in every place your life enters.

Be Blessed, Be Love, Be Light and Shine!!

Ap. Milagros Hayes
Miracles Ministries

Prayer

Father, You are an amazing God!! You wake us morning by morning and keep us through the watch of the night. How glorious and marvelous are Your ways for us. Even when we do not acknowledge Your eternal presence in our daily lives, You remain faithful in guiding, protecting, and keeping us. Thank You for showing us the depth, height, width, and length of Your love for us. We are alive yet another day, and we shall yet give You Praise!

Ap. Milagros Hayes
Miracles Ministries

Prayer & Intercession:
Successful Kingdom Event

Father, we pray over the upcoming conference. We pray souls be added to Your Kingdom by the Power of the Holy Spirit's outpouring at every gathering. Let Your love overwhelm us. I pray for those You are calling to be part of this Divine Shift. Send helpers to come alongside us to assist. I pray every detail is executed with a spirit of excellence. We release the clarion call in the Spirit to awaken those who will partake in this conference. Thank You, Father, for keeping this work fresh in our hearts and minds so that we can keep it in our prayers as we saturate the vision and atmosphere with the Glory of Your Presence. We present this conference at Your Throne of Grace. Empower us to speak Your word boldly and accompany it with signs and wonders in Yeshua's name, Amen.

Ap. Milagros Hayes
Miracles Ministries

Prayer & Intercession:
Team Members & Their Families

Father God, I pray that You bless every team member and their families. I pray You refresh and strengthen each one. For those who are battling any sickness, we declare divine healing. Let Your love abound in and through us, individually, in our families, and as a team. May our focus as Prayer warriors be on Your divine assignments to fulfill Your mandate at the altar of prayer. We pray for souls to come into the kingdom. We pray, Lord God, that You begin to open the hearts of those You desire to save and draw close to You to know and accept Jesus as Lord and Savior. We pray for salvation for those who are lost in darkness throughout this week. May our lives so shine that they will draw close to the heart of God through our witness. We are interceding for souls to flood Your altar to accept Christ Jesus as Lord. In Jesus' name, Amen.

Ap. Milagros Hayes
Miracles Ministries

Prayer & Intercession:
Team Members & Their Families

Father, in the name of Jesus, I pray for a divine refreshing, replenishing, renewing, and strengthening for each one of the team members. I pray You bless their lives, their going out, and their coming in. Bless their families and homes, businesses, children, and marriages. Father, bless the work of their hands; I declare every need is met. God, Your word says that You will provide all our needs according to Your riches in glory in Christ Jesus. Thank You for abundantly supplying to the full each one and their families. Thank You, Abba, for opening up doors of grace, favor, opportunity, and blessing. I want to thank You, Lord, for an amazing team of intercessors and prayer warriors. Fill them to the full, and replenish them in the name of Jesus. Amen.

Ap. Milagros Hayes
Miracles Ministries

Reflections

Peace, Praise & Worship

John 4:24

"It is in the process of being worshiped that God communicates His presence to men."

– *C.S. Lewis*

Reflection

The Quietness of the soul is found only in the Presence of Jehovah; there is no place quieter where one can embrace the grace of deeper communion.

Life shall not become too busy to lure me away from the secret place where there is safety for the soul.

When we master sitting alone, away from all human life and the distraction of noise, we can receive from the heartbeat of the Lord, His peace and joy.

Ap. Milagros Hayes
Miracles Ministries

Reflection

Christian maturity becomes evident, when our praise becomes unconditional.

Pastor Jerrold Snipes
Legacy Fellowship

Reflection

True worship, in spirit and in truth, grants us access to and gains the attention of our Heavenly Father.

Pastor Jerrold Snipes
Legacy Fellowship

Reflection

The experience of worship begins with our song and ends with a lifestyle that is obedient to God.

Pastor Jerrold Snipes
Legacy Fellowship

Reflections
WHISPERS OF THE SOUL©

Psalm 91:1

"Prayer is the most important activity a believer can engage in."

– *Dr. Myles Munroe*

Reflection: Whispers of the Soul©

The Whispers in my soul, the secrets of Father by Holy Spirit

It is more important to me that I have His life and nature be infused within me, His kindness and love flow inward saturating my soul. There is nothing, not even all the wealth in the world, that is more desirable than His love. I want to know all the measures of His love. I need to know Him; I want only Him.

He will ask you to be a vessel to express His love.

There is a whisper in my soul drawing me closer, where His presence encompasses me, wholly within.

Ap. Milagros Hayes
Miracles Ministries

Reflection: Whispers of the Soul©

Whisper 2

Forgiveness purges the poison of a heart's vengeance. It breaks the confinement of the soul and leads us to embrace the greatness of His love.

Love must have the ability to be dispersed; it manifests His heart, which brings wholeness and purity.

A broken and contrite heart, The Lord will not despise.

Psalm 34:18 (KJV)
The LORD is nigh unto them that are of a broken heart; and saveth such as be of a contrite spirit.

Psalm 51:17 (KJV)
The sacrifices of God are a broken spirit: a broken and a contrite heart, O God, thou wilt not despise.

Ap. Milagros Hayes
Miracles Ministries

Reflection: Whispers of the Soul©

Whisper 3
Psalm 91

Come with Me into this secret place that I have designed just for you. It's filled with Glory divine through and through. When you enter in, you will leave this world and enter into a quietness of soul. I have brought you into My secret place; not all can come; they must have the blood of My Son. The secret place can only be found if the secret has been given. Come, I invite you to go deeper, selah. There are no sounds from your world within; only the quietness of the soul can hear the sounds of the King. When I call you in, I will whisper to you the treasures of My heart, and I will fill you with My Glory to impart. Release it to all I send you to, for they all will not come to Me, and I must make known to them that I AM.

Ap. Milagros Hayes
Miracles Ministries

Reflection: Whispers of the Soul©

Whisper 4
Life Springs of Praise

There is a place in Him that is filled with a Praise that breaks shackles, lifts heaviness, conquers demonic assaults, and shuts the mouths of lions. If sought after diligently, you will be guided into this Secret Place. It's a hidden place where the waters of life flow. When you drink from this spring, eternal praise breaks forth, quenching the weary and downcast soul. It's an unexplainable praise that shouts even without sounds from the mouth. It can spread and saturate any who are near the well, releasing springs of living water to wash, mend, and heal. It's a Praise that continues even while you are asleep, for this praise was given through a breakthrough in the spirit where worship was key. Hallelujah! Hallelujah! The Living Waters of Life are filled with joy, unspeakable joy...

1 Samuel 17:26-37

Ap. Milagros Hayes
Miracles Ministries

Reflection: Whispers of the Soul©

Whispers: My Protector[1]
Psalm 31

My soul is quiet and calm, for I have been delivered from the raging storms and from the wicked tongue of evil men. My King has hidden me in His secret pavilion, where His loving kindness shields me from the snares of my enemies.

Ap. Milagros Hayes
Miracles Ministries

---

[1]*Milagros Hayes, Miracles Poetry, DRM Publishing, LLC, 2024, used with permission.*

Reflection: Whispers of the Soul©

Whispers: He Restoreth My Soul'
Psalm 23:3

My restored soul is a reflection of My King now my worship flows pure from the waters of His spring. I can now cry Holy, Holy, Holy is the Lord God Almighty that healed me and set me free.

Ap. Milagros Hayes
Miracles Ministries

¹Milagros Hayes, Miracles Poetry, DRM Publishing, LLC, 2024, used with permission.

Reflection: Whispers of the Soul©

Whispers: The Waters of Refreshing [1]
Isaiah 44:3; Psalm 23

When I was exhausted and weary, You poured water on my soul, refreshed my inner being and strengthened my weak knees.
How wonderful and glorious is Your unfailing love for me.
My soul has been replenished like green pastures by still waters.

Ap. Milagros Hayes
Miracles Ministries

[1] *Milagros Hayes, Miracles Poetry, DRM Publishing, LLC, 2024, used with permission.*

Reflection: Whispers of the Soul©

Whispers: Yeshua[1]

His love immersed my inner life; I am submerged in His realm of Glory, where there is divine solace and peace.

Every Morning has been commanded forth in the Goodness of God and The Joy of the Lord!

The Dawning of the Day

In the rising of the morning Sun as I sit quietly in the presence of My Lord; my soul cannot but express worship to Him who gives such peace in knowing He will guide and protect me as I go about my day.

Psalm 143:8

Ap. Milagros Hayes
Miracles Ministries

[1] Milagros Hayes, Miracles Poetry, DRM Publishing, LLC, 2024, used with permission.

"The prayer of intercession is an act of partnership with God to bring His will to earth."

– *Derek Prince*

Authors

Covenant Collaboration

This is a collaborative work of faith and devotion — a covenant partnership united by shared purpose and spiritual vision.

Ecclesiastes 4:9

Milagros Hayes

is a beacon of faith and inspiration, residing in San Antonio, Texas, with her beloved husband, Mr. Ronald O. Hayes. Together, they celebrate the joy of a blended family, encompassing the beauty of unity and love. Ordained as Senior Pastor of Shiloah Covenant Church by her late Spiritual Father, Bishop Richard Eberiga, Apostle Milagros has dedicated her life to serving others. Presently, she serves under Bishop Brent M. Bryant, Sr., at Redeeming Grace Church, where she has been confirmed and certified as an Apostle.

In 1998, Apostle Milagros founded **Waters of Shiloah Ministries**, a haven for authentic deliverance and inner healing. As a Women's Conference Host, Speaker, and Intercessor, she brings hope and transformation to many. . Through her diligent prayer life, she has witnessed the miraculous and established **Miracles Ministries.**

Apostle Milagros is devoted to intercession and worship, exemplifying a life rooted in Covenant and Agape Love.

https://miraclesministriesmovement.org
MiraclesPrayerMinistries@gmail.com

DIARAHA R. MCDANIELS

is the Founder and CEO of DRM Enterprise, which encompasses D. R. McDaniels, LLC, D'Opus Agency, LLC, DRM Publishing, LLC, and Call 2 Market Global, Inc. (C2M).

Passionate about empowering others to excel in the marketplace, Dee combines entrepreneurial vision, consulting expertise, and strategic insight to transform ideas into impactful realities. Her work equips individuals and organizations to align their strategies with their strengths and God-given purpose.

An ordained prophetess and dynamic teacher of the Word of God with over 25 years of ministry experience, Prophetess Dee believes true transformation begins with a renewed mindset rooted in biblical principles. Known for ministering "Paradigm Shift," she emphasizes mindset alignment with the Word of God to drive lasting spiritual, personal, and professional change.

At C2M, Dee bridges spiritual growth with professional and personal development, offering innovative solutions and strategic guidance to help clients overcome challenges and achieve sustainable success. Certified in project management, change management, and Lean Six Sigma, she excels in enhancing processes, managing risks, and leading transformational initiatives.

Dee continues to make a significant impact through her leadership, mentorship, and ministry, empowering others to thrive holistically by blending faith with practical strategies.

HTTPS://DRMCDENTERPRISE.COM

Jerrold Snipes

is a passionate leader at Legacy Fellowship, where he has dedicated the past 10 years as Senior Pastor. Alongside his ministry, he has excelled as a Service Technician for AT&T for over 11 years, earning the recognition of Employee of the Month multiple times for his commitment to excellence.

With a diverse ministerial background, Pastor Jerrold has served as a Lead Pastor, Assistant Pastor, and Worship Pastor. He embodies a heart of worship and a deep commitment to serving others. His experience in the marketplace includes roles such as Service Manager for Al Gardner and owner of J. Tech Communications, showcasing his ability to lead and inspire both in the church and the business world.

An ordained pastor, Pastor Jerrold is dedicated to lifelong learning and holds certifications in Avaya and CCNA. His journey reflects a deep commitment to personal and professional growth, which he uses to empower those around him.

With a heart for ministry, Pastor Jerrold is not just a leader but also a father in the faith, inspiring others through his writings and music. As a talented musician and published songwriter, he uses his gifts to uplift and encourage his congregation, reminding them of the transformative power of worship.

Guided by the principle found in Luke 6:38 (NIV) - "Give, and it will be given to you. A good measure, pressed down, shaken together, and running over, will be poured into your lap. For with the measure you use, it will be measured to you." - Pastor Jerrold believes in the profound impact of generosity and the blessings that flow from a giving spirit. He finds joy in seeing others thrive and is deeply committed to nurturing his community.

In his personal life, Jerrold treasures time spent with his beloved wife, Jessica, and their two children, Benjamin and Leah. Together, they create a loving home that reflects their faith and commitment to serving others. With an unwavering belief in the power of love and service, Pastor Jerrold Snipes inspires all those around him to live purposefully and make a difference in the world.

Legacy Fellowship
11610 El Sendero
San Antonio, TX 78233
(210) 716-2808

Sunday Service - 10:30 AM CT

LF-SA.org
https://www.facebook.com/legacyfellowshipsa
LegacyFellowship@gmail.com

www.ingramcontent.com/pod-product-compliance
Lightning Source LLC
LaVergne TN
LVHW010315070426
835510LV00024B/3398